How to Live a Life of Miracles

Miracles

*7 Keys to Open Yourself
to Blessings, Wholeness & Happiness*

BO SANCHEZ

#1 Bestselling Aurhor of *40 Stories of Passion*

How to Live a Life of Miracles
7 Keys to Open Yourself to Blessings, Wholeness & Happiness

ISBN- ISBN 978-971-007-000-8

BO SANCHEZ

Requests for information should be addressed to:
SHEPHERD'S VOICE PUBLICATIONS, INC.
#60 Chicago St., Cubao, Quezon City, Philippines 1109
P.O. Box 1331 Quezon City Central Post Office
1153 Quezon City
Tel. No. (+632) 411-7874 to 77; Fax. No. (632) 727-5615
e-mail: sale@shepherdsvoice.com.ph

Layout and design by Rey de Guzman

Table of Contents

An Introduction

You're a Walking, Talking, Breathing, Living Miracle

A Billion Things Had to Happen in a Precise Order for You to Be Here, Alive, Reading This Book, Right Now!

May I share with you two beautiful love stories?

It began not too long ago.

In March 16, 1521, when Magellan came to the Philippine islands...

Let me skip a few centuries and fast forward to 1910.

Her name was Magdalena. Her father was a full-blooded Spaniard.

Being half-Spanish, she was a *mestiza*. A beautiful *mestiza*.

A young *Pinoy*[1] named Tomas fell in love with the lovely Magdalena.

He courted her, but he had a major problem. He couldn't even communicate well with her parents. He couldn't speak Spanish. Except for a few words, the words all of us know, like *pastillas de leche, agua oxigenada,* and *poso negro.* But that didn't stop him from pursuing her.

However, his first visit to Magdalena's home was a total disaster.

---

[1] Filipino

When Magdalena's father asked him, *"¿Que quieres comer?* (What do you want to eat?), Tomas didn't understand a thing. So he just smiled and muttered the Spanish words he knew. Tomas said, *"Pastillas de leche."*[2]

When the father of Magdalena asked him, *"¿Que quieres beber?* (What do you want to drink?), Tomas answered, *"Agua oxigenada."*[3]

Magdalena's father scratched his head, wondering who this guy was. So he asked him, *"¿Donde vives?* (Where do you live?), Tomas was at a total loss as to what to say, so he just said the last Spanish words he knew. *"Poso negro."*[4]

I'm just kidding. I made this whole conversation up.

What really happened was Magdalena's parents rejected Tomas. During that time, a parent's word was the final word.

Poor Tomas. Broken-hearted, he went to Hong Kong to work and forget the pain of losing Magdalena forever.

A Marriage to Another Man

A new suitor came into the picture: Pablo.

Pablo was a doctor. More importantly, he was *mestizo* and spoke Spanish. And he was accepted by Magdalena's parents right away.

And in a few months, Pablo married Magdalena.

But soon, Magdalena woke up to a harsh reality. Just a few months after her wedding, she discovered that her husband Pablo was a hopeless womanizer. He would have many, many affairs. His infidelities would wound her heart again and again for the next 13 years.

And then, suddenly, tragedy struck.

One day, a seemingly raving madman entered the clinic of Dr. Pablo. In his hand was a sharp knife. He had only one intention — to kill the doctor.

Pablo ran to the street. But he wasn't fast enough. In a busy intersection in Manila, Pablo was stabbed to death.

---

[2] Milk candy
[3] Hydrogen peroxide
[4] Septic Tank

Later on, they established the motive of the murder. Revenge and jealousy, because Pablo was having an affair with the man's wife.

Love Is Sweeter the Second Time Around

Tomas was in Hong Kong when he heard of the gruesome news.

Even after 13 long years, he was never able to forget Magdalena. When he learned of the tragedy, he packed his things and took the next ship back to Manila.

On that fateful morning, Magdalena couldn't believe her eyes when she opened the door. There in front of her, at her doorstep, was a man she once loved many, many years ago.

But for Tomas, it was very different. He had never stopped loving her.

So he courted her again.

And he won her heart again.

After one year, they got married.

They only had one child.

And they named her Pilar.

An Office Love Affair

In 1944, during the Japanese war, Pilar was a shy 19-year-old girl when she applied for a job in one of the small offices in Manila.

And that was where she met Gene for the very first time.

Twenty-five-year-old Gene watched this beautiful young lady come into his office. He was in charge of interviewing new applicants and giving them a qualifying exam.

During her exam, Pilar was surprised because her examiner was giving her the answers to the test.

After the test, Gene asked Pilar for their first-ever romantic date. He said, "Pilar, will you join me at the 6:00 a.m. Mass tomorrow?"

That was an incredibly unique date if you ask me.

And so every morning, they went to church.

And here's the juicy part of their story: Three weeks later, they got married!

My jaw fell to the floor when I first learned about it. Pilar and Gene kept this little secret from me until I was in my 20s. I asked, "Mom! Why in the world did you get married so quickly?" (Yep, Pilar and Gene are my parents. And Tomas and Magdalena are my grandparents.)

Mom blushed, "Oh, because of your father."

Dad smiled. "Times were different then. It was the Japanese war. One didn't know if he'd still be alive the next day. And besides, your mother had another suitor — I wanted to make the competition irrelevant."

And then it hit me.

Wow, what if Mom married the other suitor?

You wouldn't be reading this book. Because the author would never have existed!

It Took a Dizzying Number of Events to Make You — You!

I had other curious questions.

What if Tomas married someone else in Hong Kong?

Or what if Tomas never pursued Magdalena the second time around? Mom would never have existed.

Or what if Dad was absent that day when Mom took the exam — and she failed? (No offense, Mom. Totally hypothetical.)

Or what if Mom applied in another company — and they never met each other?

Or what if Mom and Dad died in the Japanese war before they had kids?

Or what if Mom and Dad never had another kid after their fifth child? (I'm the sixth.)

I have no great theological answers to all these questions.

But I do know one thing.

If these things happened, I would not be alive today.

I realize now that a billion things had to happen in a precise order for me to be here.

My point? *The fact that I exist is already a miracle.*

Hey, you, too!

Think of all the things that had to take place for you to be here, alive, reading this book right now.

You and I are a walking, talking, breathing, living miracle!

Awaken the Miracle That Is You

You are the greatest miracle that God has given to you.

Your soul. Your spirit. Your body. Your giftedness. Your past, present and future.

The way you're made up is fantastic!

And even what seemingly were mistakes of your past — God can transform for your good.

The Bible says you're God's workmanship.

My paraphrase? You're God's miracle.

Many times, you don't see that.

You only see your problems. Your failures. Your faults.

Don't do that.

Look at how incredibly special you are.

In this book, I invite you to see yourself as a great miracle.

And to start living a life of miracles every day!

How to Live a Life of Miracles

Yes, it's possible.

You can live a life of miracles every day.

In this book, I'll share with you seven simple yet powerful keys on how to live a life of miracles. Here they are:

Key 1: Don't be Afraid to Ask
Key 2: Prophesy Your Future
Key 3: Bless Your Loved Ones

Key 4: Proclaim Who You Are

Key 5: Have Trials? Stand Up and Walk

Key 6: Take Out the Trash

Key 7: Sow in Times of Famine

Let me remind you: You're not only a miracle yourself, but you're also living in a world of miracles. In God's universe, there is no shortage of miracles.

But unless you *open* yourself to that world of miracles, you won't taste any of it.

How do you open up? I'll tell you.

May your dreams come true,

Bo Sanchez

P.S. Sign up at www.BoSanchez.ph for my FREE weekly Soulfood Letter. Thousands write to me and tell me this blog has changed their lives.

P.S. If you want to gain financial abundance without robbing your soul, log on to www.IAmTrulyRich.com for my FREE TrulyRich Letter. You'll be enriched by the practical wisdom and inspiration on how to gain financial freedom so you can serve God with your life and money. Sign up now!

P.S. For a stronger spiritual life, join our virtual community at www. KerygmaFamily.com for FREE. Get a spiritual support system so you can grow closer to God.

KEY 1

Don't Be Afraid to Ask

Get Rid of the 4 Inner Blocks That Prevent You from Receiving Your Blessings

You create your opportunities by asking for them.
— Patty Hansen

Your name is already written on every blessing designated for your life.

CHAPTER 1

Don't Settle For Crumbs

I felt like a kid from a third world country, preaching in my first US Catholic Convention.

So I was thrilled and nervous at the same time.

Nervous because I was going to preach to Americans. (Will they listen to a brown-skinned *Pinoy?*[1] Will they understand my jokes?) Nervous because most of the other speakers were big-time American bishops and priests. And nervous because I was in my 20s, their youngest speaker.

I felt small, young and ignorant.

After my talk (that turned out very well), the convention broke up for lunch. Participants made a beeline to the door, scattering to the different restaurants around.

Being a poor *Pinoy*, I decided to save money. I spotted a quiet corner in the hall, sat down on the carpeted floor and munched my biscuits. That was my lunch and I was happy.

The next day, I preached another talk.

And again, during lunchtime, I did the exact same thing: I found my quiet corner, sat on the floor and ate my biscuit.

And that was when one of the organizers saw me and almost shouted, "There you are! I've been looking for you. Brother Bo, what are you doing there sitting on the floor?"

[1] Filipino

Your Name Is Already Written on Every Blessing Designated for Your Life

"Eating my lunch," I smiled.

"But Brother Bo, we have lunch prepared for all the speakers. The bishops and the other speakers are waiting for you!"

Now I kind of figured that the organizers would prepare lunch for the bishops. But for me, too? Nah. I was this kid from the Philippines.

But when she escorted me to the dining room — lo and behold — it was a huge buffet! There was a long table filled with food. There were five main dishes with two desserts and waiters serving drinks.

And to my greater surprise, on top of the table was a little card with my name on it, "Bo Sanchez — Speaker." It had been waiting for me all along.

The bishop beside my seat asked, "Hey, Brother Bo, where were you yesterday? No one sat on your seat."

How could I tell him, "Bishop, to save money, I was sitting in some dark corner, munching on my biscuits that my mother packed for me from Manila"?

Why did I miss the buffet?

Here's why: *Because I didn't ask.*

All I had to do was ask the organizers, "Excuse me, do you have lunch prepared for the speakers?"

I didn't ask because I was afraid to ask.

And I believe the same thing happens in our lives.

There's a Buffet of Blessings Waiting for You!

Many times we miss out on God's blessings.

We're sitting on the floor in some corner munching on a tiny biscuit when there's a glorious buffet waiting for us — a Buffet of Blessings. God has prepared this banquet for us — a feast with our name on it.

Why are we not enjoying God's Buffet?

Because we don't know it's there.

Because we're *afraid* to be rejected at the table.

Because we feel we're not worthy to even ask.

We're content with our biscuit-sized blessings.

Friend, if you've been subsisting on crackers and missing out on the feast, believe me, I understand where you're coming from.

But you don't have to stay in that corner forever. That's why I'm sharing this book with you.

There are four *inner blocks* that prevent you from receiving your blessings.

Identify them, get rid of them and start enjoying your *buffet of blessings!*

Many people ask
for nothing.
And consequently,
they end up
getting it.

CHAPTER 2

Inner Block #1: You Don't Specify What You Want

I love talking to kids.

Especially tiny ones.

When I ask kids age 3, 4 or 5, "What do you want to be when you grow up?" the most common answer I get is, "I don't know." That's understandable. They're still figuring out what they want in life. (But I keep asking this question anyway to help them start envisioning their future.)

But when I ask adults in their 30s, 40s and 50s what they want in life, the most common answer I get is still, "I don't know."

This I don't understand. Half of their life is over and they still don't know what they want.

Here's the problem: If you want nothing, you get nothing.

Oftentimes, when I ask single women what they want, the answer is, "To get married!"

I've met many single women whose simple prayer is, "Lord, give me a husband."

So I ask them, "Any husband? Isn't that too general?" And with a laugh, they answer, "Yes, Bo. I'm desperate. Any husband will do."

And that's what they get: any husband.

Which is pretty dangerous if you ask me.

You Get What You Settle For

One of the craziest emails I've ever received was from a single woman who wrote, "Brother Bo, I caught my boyfriend cheating on me twice with another girl. What should I do? Should I break up with him? But the thing is, he's really a good person."

I wanted to say, "Good? He was unfaithful to you two times and you call him good?"

In another email, a single woman asked me, "Brother Bo, my boyfriend is a drunkard. When he gets drunk, he gets violent and beats me up. Brother Bo, what should I do? Because when he's not drunk, he's a really good person."

For some people, "good" means someone who doesn't kill you with a butcher knife.

When you pray for a spouse, don't just ask for a "good" husband or a "good" wife. Because "good" can mean so many things.

Be specific!

Say, "I want a husband who is faithful. A husband who is responsible. A husband who is financially stable. A husband who is free from addictions and alcoholism...."

I can hear you now: "But Bo, you've just scratched off 99% of the men I know!"

Then that simply means you're hanging out with the wrong crowd.

Here's my message: Don't settle!

Because you get what you settle for. (I discuss this more fully in my book, *How to Find Your One True Love,* Book 1 and Book 2.)

How Much Do You Want?

Hey, I found that this works with money as well.

Here's my belief: God has programmed His entire creation to give us what we clearly and specifically ask for.

So if you ask, "Give me money," God's creation will be asking, "How much?"

The universe could deliver to you 25 cents or $25 million. Both are money. So be specific.

Each year, I write down a financial goal. In fact, I know how much I'll be earning every single year for the next 20 years. I pray for it every day.

The universe responds to someone who passionately knows what he wants and wants it with specificity. Don't ask in ignorance. Ask with knowledge.

Know what you want.

Define it.

Be specific.

And don't settle.

Many people ask for nothing.

And consequently, they end up getting it.

Many times, we don't ask because we think we don't deserve to ask.

CHAPTER 3

Inner Block #2:
You Feel Shame for Who
You Are

There are people who feel that they don't deserve to ask for anything.

That's why I like the story of Elijah and Elisha.[2]

Next to Moses, Elijah was the greatest Old Testament prophet. Elisha was his disciple, his understudy. Think Robin to Batman.

One day, the great prophet says to his disciple, "Ask what I shall do for you before I be taken away from you."

I love what Elisha said. He replied, "I pray that I get a double portion of your spirit."

Wow! What guts. What daring. What boldness!

Sometimes, I imagine if Elisha was Filipino. It would have been a very different scenario, believe me.

Because the *Pinoy* Elisha would have blushed, chuckled and with a wave of his hand replied, "Oh, nothing at all. You've given me so much already."

And Elijah would have to cajole him, "Come on, Elisha, tell me. What do you want?"

To which the *Pinoy* Elisha would reply, "Nothing. Really! Nothing at all."

---

[2] 2 Kings 2:9-10

Elijah would press some more, until Elisha would say, "OK, just give me an itsy-bitsy, little, tiny smudge of your anointing. And I'll be more than happy!"

This is what I call the "Itsy-bitsy Spirituality." And it has many devotees.

It's very Filipino. But I'm sure that it's a universal phenomenon, too.

We need to learn to ask.

Many times, we don't ask because we think we don't deserve to ask.

We don't feel we deserve a good job.

We don't feel we deserve a good husband.

We don't feel we deserve a house.

We don't feel we deserve healing.

We think that we're small.

CHAPTER 4

Inner Block #3:
You're Afraid of What Others
Will Say

When we hear prayers like Elijah's, it seems selfish.

If there were people around who heard Elisha asking for a double portion, perhaps some of them would have said, "How dare he ask that way? My gosh, he asked for double. The gall. How arrogant! How selfish!"

But Elijah asked for a double portion not so that he would be greater than his teacher. No. He asked so that he could serve more. (So if you're going to ask, might as well ask big.)

Some people are afraid of rejection. They're scared that when they're successful, their family and friends will say, "You're different now." So they don't ask for what God wants to give them. "What will other people say?" they think. So the Buffet of Blessings is waiting but they don't partake of it because of shame.

There are times when we pray for something, and then we stop because we feel that it's a selfish prayer. "It's just for me," we think. And so we reject the blessing of God that was supposed to be — not for us — but to be used as a blessing for many others.

Here's a key principle you've got to understand: God wants to bless others through you, but He has to bless you first.

God wants us to ask! And when we do, we should expect to get it.

CHAPTER 5

Inner Block #4: You've Got Wrong Beliefs about God

This is the biggest block. And many of us have wrong beliefs! Here are some of them:

- **Myth #1: God is stingy.**
  For crying out loud, how can God be stingy?

  Just watch one episode of Discovery Channel and you get the incredible idea that God is a recklessly, incurably generous Being. The vastness of the oceans. The different species of plants, animals, insects — it's mind-boggling. Goodness, we don't even know how many galaxies there are in the universe.

- **Myth #2: The world is cruel, hard and selfish.**
  Some people are paranoid. When they walk down a road, every person that looks at them for more than two seconds is either a serial killer or a drug-crazed rapist.

  Some people are paranoid about life in general. These people also wake up in the morning and think, "What misfortune will befall me today?"

  There's such a thing as *inverse paranoid,* and that's me.

  I wake up in the morning and I expect good things to happen to me.

And I expect people to be good and kind. This is my default thinking. I go to a gathering and I expect that everyone is happy and loving and that they'll like me. Isn't that a much better way to live?

- **Myth #3: If I'm really a good person, I'll live a life of suffering.**
One day, I met a woman we'll call Sally. She said, "Brother Bo, please pray for me. My marriage is a mess. My husband is terrible. My children are problematic — one got pregnant out of wedlock and the other is into drugs. Financially, we're really hard up. And to top it all, I'm sick. I have ulcers, hypertension…. Oh, Bo, I have so many trials."

So I asked, "What do you want me to pray for?"

"Endurance. That's all. That God would give me the strength to carry all my burdens," she replied.

I was impressed. How saintly.

"Anything else?" I asked.

"That's all," she said, adding, "I've gotten used to all this."

That's when I wondered. Was she really holy? (It was possible.) Or was she rejecting God's blessings because she felt closer to Him in her suffering? Unconsciously, did she believe that good people live miserable lives while bad people live happy lives?

Don't get me wrong. I believe that we can feel the presence of God in our trials. That's a great fact. But I also believe that a normal, healthy person doesn't want to suffer uselessly.

- **Myth #4: A decent person doesn't ask; it's shameful to ask.**
There are people who think that the mere act of asking is wrong.

Jamie, an educated woman, had an unconscious belief that it was shameful to ask for anything.

Imagine this scenario: One day, Jamie asks, "Mom, can you give me a doll?"

Her mother screams, "Who do you think you are, asking for a doll? I work long hours to pay off our debts. I go home to cook and do the laundry. And here you are asking me for a doll? You only think of yourself. You don't think of how difficult it is to earn money. How dare you! You should be ashamed of yourself."

And so Jamie grew up not asking for anything. In her heart of hearts, she believed that it was a sin to ask. So she never asked again. Even from God.

But Jesus tells us, "Until now you have asked nothing in my name. Ask, so that you will receive, that your joy may be full."[3]

God wants us to ask! And when we do, we should expect to get it.

Bestselling author Norman Vincent Peale says, "We tend to get what we expect." And Jesus Himself said, "Therefore I tell you, whatever you ask in prayer, believe that you have received it, and it will be yours."[4]

When I look at my kids, I believe we need to relearn this skill of asking.

---

[3] John 16:24
[4] Mark 11:24

God is telling you, "My child, the blessings are here. It's waiting for you. Stand up! Ask for a double portion!"

Chapter 6

Relearn the Skill of Asking

When he was barely two years old, my little boy Francis couldn't pronounce the word "milk." Instead, he would say, "Mi." So whenever he wanted milk, he'd say "mi." But like any child, he'd say it a million times if necessary until he gets it.

And if you hear, "Mi. Mi. Mi. Mi. Mi. Mi..." over and over again, you'll really give him what he wants.

My eldest son, Bene, who's eight now, also knows how to ask. But because he's a bit older, he asks with sophistication. He makes it easier for you to say yes.

One suppertime, he asked his mother, "After dinner, can I play on the computer?"

My wife replied, "Son, read a book."

My son's facial expression didn't change. With a big happy smile, he asked, "Mommy, after I read the book, can I play on the computer?"

My wife answered, "Son, after you read the book, go straight to bed."

Again, still with the grin on his face, he asked, "Mommy, after I read the book, before I go to bed, can I play the computer for 30 minutes?"

My wife said, "No, I want you to sleep right away."

"Mommy, how about if I play just for 15 minutes?"

"No, I want you to go to bed right away."

"Mommy, how about 10 minutes? Just 10 minutes? Please, please, please?"

"Owwwwww... OK!" my wife conceded.

Now that's the power of asking.

My son expected to get what he wanted.

He used his smile. He used compromise. He used his puppy eyes. He used his cuteness. But the important thing was he got what he wanted.

The Universe Adjusts to Your Expectations

As adults, we don't do that anymore. We don't ask with expectancy.

So we go to God and say, "Lord, please give me...." And when we don't get it, we say, "OK, never mind."

We quit. Easily.

Here's the problem: The universe adjusts to your expectations.

If you expect nothing, you get nothing.

The universe is the greatest Buffet of Blessings. Don't settle for a biscuit. Don't eat crumbs in a dark corner of your life.

God is telling you, "My child, the blessings are here. It's waiting for you. Stand up! Ask. Not for a bit. Not for a little. Ask for a double portion!"

Are you ready to ask?

KEY 2

Prophesy Your Future

Use the Power of Your Words to Paint a Picture of Your Desired Destiny

It's a funny thing about life.
If you refuse to accept anything but the best,
you very often get it.
— Somerset Maugham

Prophesy your
future with
the power of
thought and the
power of words.

CHAPTER 7

A Prophecy That Changed My Life

When I was 13 years old, something magical happened.

One day, Aida, our prayer group leader, a mother of six children, told me, "God whispered something about you when I was praying last night. God said that you shall receive the gift of wisdom and you'll preach all over the world."

Imagine that moment.

At 13, I was small. I was thin. I was ugly. (I know that's a little bit difficult to imagine now...) What in the world did she see in me?

She saw something that others, not even myself, saw.

How did she know?

Fast forward to the present: I've been preaching for 30 years now. And to date, I've preached in 14 countries all over the world.

This is why I believe that God has given us the power to prophesy our future with the power of thought and the power of words.

Write down your dream with a heart committed to make it come true, and your words will determine your future.

CHAPTER 8

Words Can Affect Your Future

Jim Carrey used to be a struggling standup comedian in some small comedy bar. But he believed in the power of words. He wrote out a check to himself for $10 million. Underneath it he wrote, "For services rendered."

When he slept, he pasted it on his ceiling so that the check would be the first thing he'd see when he woke up. Then he'd put it in his wallet where he'd see it every time he pulled it out. Today, Jim Carrey receives $20 million or more for every movie he makes.

Words are powerful because thoughts are powerful. And words are more powerful than thoughts because words are thoughts expressed. And written words are more powerful than words because written words are thoughts expressed permanently. You actually write it down and you see it in black and white.

Jim Carrey didn't use the words prophecy but that's basically what happened. He prophesied his future.

Write Your Dreams Down

Suze Orman, the bestselling author of *9 Steps to Financial Freedom,* began as an ordinary saleswoman. But she was always terrified that she wouldn't meet her quota.

So she decided to use the power of her words. She sat down and wrote, "I will be a young successful saleswoman. I will sell $10,000 every single month."

She did this every day, many times a day. Soon, she was selling more than $10,000 a month.

Using the same strategy, she's now become a bestselling author, radio and TV host, and international speaker. All by the power of writing down her dream.

Do It Many Times a Day!

My third example is Scott Adams, creator of the Dilbert comics. He used to be an office employee working in a small cubicle who doodled all day.

Then one morning, he decided, "I'm going to commit myself to my dream." He sat down and wrote on a piece of paper: "I will be a syndicated cartoonist." A syndicated cartoonist writes a comic strip that appears in many newspapers. He wrote down his dream 15 times a day, every day.

He made a comic strip and submitted it to newspapers only to be rejected again and again. "It's no good," they'd comment. "It's not funny enough," they said.

But Scott didn't give up. Then one day, a newspaper accepted his comic strip. And another. And many more followed. It was a sweet victory for him.

But now that he was a syndicated cartoonist, he said, "OK, I'm gonna change what I write." He wrote a new line, "I will be the best cartoonist on the planet." He wrote this 15 times a day too, every single day.

Today, Dilbert appears in 2,000 newspapers worldwide.

Friends, this is the power of words written down on paper. Write it with a heart committed to make that dream come true, and your words will determine your future.

CHAPTER 9

Negative Words
Have Power, Too

But while positive words affect your future, so do negative ones.

I once worked with a guy in a ministry many, many years ago. Every once in a while, I'd get a crazy idea and say, "I have a new proposal." Even before I could expound on my idea, this man would be shaking his head. "That won't work," he'd say.

His name was Norman, and because everyone knew he was that kind of a guy, we called him Negative Norman.

It was so difficult to work with him. One time, everyone liked my proposal except Negative Norman. The team implemented my proposal and it was a great success. We all wondered what Negative Norman had to say.

In our next meeting, everyone was raving about the successful project. Norman was there with his usual frown and he said, "That won't last. I tell you, you can't sustain it."

You know what happened? The project continued and became even more successful. We wondered what Norman would say this time.

At our next meeting, he was there, still with his usual frown. He said, "You know, Bo, you're becoming proud. You've become so different."

I couldn't believe how negative this person was.

One of the things I realized is if you say you can't do it, you're absolutely right. *You cannot do it!*

Words Affect Your Health

Your words not only affect your future, it affects your health as well.

I had a friend who'd always say, "I'm gonna die. I'm dying soon. And when I'm grasping for breath on my deathbed, please don't even try to revive me."

His words became a self-fulfilling prophecy. Before he reached 60, my friend suddenly died of a heart attack. Words are so powerful that if you keep on saying it, you create its reality.

Someone asked me, "Bo, my uncle seemed like he had a premonition that he would die. The day before his death, he said, 'I bid you farewell now.' He said his goodbyes and the next day, he was dead! Did he have a premonition, Bo?"

Many times, it's not a premonition. It's prophecy at work.

There were reports that in some American Indian tribes, it was customary that an elderly member would gather his children and grandchildren to say goodbye. He would say, "I'm passing on to the next world. Goodbye!" He would then enter his tent, sleep and die. It was almost like he willed himself to death.

Friends, we have more power over our bodies and our lives than we think we have — through our thoughts and words.

CHAPTER 10

It's in Your Brain

Let me explain to you why writing down your dreams works. Have you ever had this experience?

You're in a party. It's noisy. Lots of chatter, laughter and loud music. But from the other side of the room, you hear someone whisper your name.

Thank your reticular activating system (or RAS) for this phenomenon. It's a filtering mechanism at the base of your brain that sorts through the entire tidal wave of visual, sensory and auditory stimuli you receive.

The RAS is also what allows a mother to sleep through the noise of cars honking outside her home. The RAS tells her to ignore these irrelevant sounds. But the second her baby cries, she's up. This time, the RAS dictates, "That's important. Wake up!"

Let me give you another example.

When my wife was pregnant some years ago, we were strolling in a mall. She said to me, "Bo, did you notice that there are so many pregnant women here, much more than before?" I just laughed because it wasn't true. Since she was pregnant, her RAS focused on all the expecting mothers who were walking around the mall. When she wasn't pregnant, she wasn't noticing them.

It's the same thing when you write down your dreams. Your RAS zeroes in on the many things that will contribute to the fulfillment of that dream.

You'll See the Ingredients of Your Dream Fall into Place Like a Jigsaw Puzzle Right Before Your Eyes

Someone asked me, "When I pray, can't I just say, 'Lord, just give me whatever You want to bless me with'? Why do we have to specify what we want?"

Sure you can pray that way.

But I think there should be times when we pray with more specificity. When I do, I see the ingredients that I need fall into place like a jigsaw puzzle right before my eyes.

Recently, I had this crazy, wonderful idea of creating a Christian computer game. I was excited and told my team about it one morning. "We're going to use a computer game to tell kids about God's love and how to love Him back!"

And like magic, that same afternoon, I received an email that said, "Brother Bo, I want to volunteer my services. I edit computer games."

What was happening? If I didn't have a dream, if I didn't pray for it, if it wasn't something that I was envisioning for my future, I would not see this was a piece of the jigsaw puzzle falling in place.

So write down your dream. Put down on paper what you want to happen in your life and present it to God.

CHAPTER 11

Remember Your Dreams by Putting Them on Paper

Finally, writing it down makes you remember your dreams.

One day, a 75-year-old golfer came home and complained to his wife, "Sweetheart, I could have played a good game today if not for my bad eyesight. After I hit the ball, I don't see where it goes."

His wife replied, "Of course your eyes are bad. After all, you're 75. So bring your older brother along."

The man said, "But he's already 85."

"It doesn't matter," the wife said, "his eyes are still good."

So the man brought his older brother to his golf game the next day. After he hit the ball, he said to his brother, "I didn't see where the ball went. Did you?"

"Yes, I did," answered the older man.

"Oh, good. Where did the ball go?"

"What ball?" asked the older man.

"The ball I just hit," replied the golfer.

"Did you hit a ball?"

The older brother had good vision but he was forgetful.

You may have a good vision and dreams for your life, but you can be forgetful.

So commit your dreams to writing. When you do, you don't forget and your RAS focuses on the blessings that come your way. When you have a dream, you attract to your life all the ingredients that you need to fulfill it.

My Story

I was so overwhelmed when I read my old journals.

In January 1992, I wrote, "I will have a daily radio program. I will have a weekly TV show that will proclaim God's love."

What were just words on a page many years ago is true today. Every day I preach God's Word on Radyo Veritas. And we have — not one — but three weekly shows airing on TV today.

Oh, I can go on and on and on. About envisioning Anawim, our ministry for the poorest of the poor. About dreaming of writing bestselling books even if I got an F in Essay Writing in English 103. About imagining my various businesses.

When I write in my journal, I don't only talk about the past. Instead, I prophesy about the future. God says, "Faith is the substance of things hoped for, the evidence of things not seen."[5]

It's your turn.

Prophesy your future.

Take a pen and paper and start writing down your dreams.

---

[5] Hebrews 11:1

KEY 3

Bless Your Loved Ones

Use Your Words to Prophesy Their Future, Too

You will have to live with the consequences of everything you say.
What you say can preserve life or destroy it.
— Proverbs 18:20, 21

When we bless
someone with
our words, we
give love. And
when we curse,
we take away
love.

CHAPTER 12

Bless or Curse, It's Up to You

May I share this with you?

My friend sent it to me and I found it... uh... enlightening...
I think.

What I Learned from My Mother
(Anonymous)

* My mother taught me about *Priorities.* Because when my brother and I fought, she'd usually say, "If you want to kill each other, go outside because I just cleaned the house."

* My mother also taught me about *Religion.* Because whenever I soiled her carpet, she'd say, "Start praying that I can remove this stain or I will chop your head off."

* My mother also taught me about *Logic.* She liked saying to me, "Here's why you need to do it. *Because I said so!*"

* My mother also taught me about *Contortionism.* When I came from school sweaty and dirty, she often told me, "My gosh, you're filthy! And look at the dirt at the back of your neck. Look at it!"

* My mother taught me the meaning of *Genetics.* She often said, "You really took after your no-good father!"

- And the favorite lesson I learned from Mom is what *Justice* is all about. She often told me, "One day, you'll have kids of your own. I pray they'll be just as stubborn and hard-headed as you are…"

A Very Strange Story

Poor guy — whoever wrote that piece above.

According to the Bible, words aren't syllables bunched up together. Words can impact the future lives of others.

Let me tell you an old — and weird — story.

Old, blind Isaac had two sons, Esau and Jacob.

When Isaac felt he was dying, he called his eldest son Esau. He said, "Hunt me some animal and cook me a hearty meal. I'm going to give you my personal blessing before I die."

As Esau ran off, he didn't notice that his mother, Rebekah, was eavesdropping.

She called Jacob, her favorite son, and explained everything to him. "Quick!" she said, "Get two goats from our flock. I'll cook them and you give the meal to your father. He'll give you a personal blessing!"

Jacob went off and did as was told. Now believe me, it's much quicker to get goats from your own flock than to hunt for a wild boar from the wilderness.

So Jacob went to his father and said, "I'm Esau. Here's the meal. Can you bless me now?"

Remember that Isaac was now almost blind. So he gave his blessing.

That was when Esau ran in with his meal. And his father said, "Alas! Your brother Jacob fooled me. I have no more blessing to give you!"

Strange story, right?

What's the Fuss About a Few Syllables?

If there's anything you learn from this story, it's this: Parents, don't ever play favorites! When you do, you may just create a war that will curse your great-great-great-great grandchildren.

The Middle East conflict between Israel and the Arab world is one of the most complex schisms in the history of the world. But you can trace it back to this crazy story — an event that took place more than 3,000 years ago.

But I want to focus on something else: What's the big hullabaloo over a personal blessing from a sick old man?

Why were Jacob and Esau fighting over words? Syllables? Sound from the lips of a dying father? Because the ancients understood what we moderns don't — *that words create reality.*

According to Genesis, God created the entire universe by speaking it forth. "Let there be light!" He said, and there was light.

Why Words Are Powerful

Parents, be careful of what you say to your kids. Because your words *prophesy* their future.

If you don't believe me, try this 10-year experiment.

Starting today, shout to your kids, "You're hard-headed!" Do this daily for the next 10 years. Believe me, your children will grow up to be the most bull-headed kids in the world.

Why do words have power?

Because love is the greatest force on this planet — and words have the capacity to either give or take away love. When we bless someone with our words, we give love. And when we curse, we take away love.

That's why words are powerful.

Catch your kids
doing good
things — and
praise them.

CHAPTER 13

Learn to Bless by Praise

There are two kinds of parents.

Parents who bless and parents who curse.

What kind of parent are you?

Face it, your kids will always make mistakes.

So here's a million-dollar advice: Choose your battles.

Many parents simply have too many battles with their children: Untidy room. Loud music. Low grades. Ugly penmanship. The list is endless.

But if your child's mistake is something that's not morally evil, let it slide!

Instead, correct only when he cheats, or lies, or does something sinful.

But if your kid is just acting like a child — he's restless, he's importunate, he's noisy, he's clumsy, he's disorganized — don't get mad at him!

I repeat: Choose your battles well. Because at the end of the day, you want to praise your children more than you correct them by a ratio of 4:1. You need to praise your child at least four times more than you correct them.

Here's the key. Stop catching your kids doing "bad" stuff. You only reinforce this behavior. Instead, catch your kids doing good things — and praise them. *What gets attention gets repeated.* And as the good grows exponentially, it displaces the bad spontaneously.

When you praise your children, you bless them.

When you praise
the people that
you love, you're
actually blessing
them.

CHAPTER 14

Do It for the Rest of the Family

The literal meaning of the word "blessing" is "to bow down." When I bow down in front of someone, I give that person value. I say to him, "You're important." And the easiest way to do that is through praise.

When you praise the people that you love, you're actually blessing them.

Here's my advice: Praise the members of your family at least once a day!

Husbands, make it a habit to praise your wife.

Let's say she's fixing herself in the mirror or closing the last button of her blouse and you happen to pass by. Stop and say, "You're so beautiful."

Or your wife prepared your meal and you take your first bite. Stop and say, "This is delicious!" Then hold her hand, look into her eyes and say, "I thank God I married you."

Wives, do the same to your husbands.

When I come home from work, many times, my wife would wrap her arms around me and tell me, "You're a great husband. You're a great father. And I'm the luckiest girl in the world."

I receive praise from thousands of people — my readers, my audience, my listeners. But for some reason, I still look to my wife to affirm me.

Some people say, "I don't have to praise my family because they already know that I appreciate them."

That's not true. You need to say it.

My friend Ces is almost 30.

Yet to this day, she still feels like a little girl who's still trying to earn the praise of her parents. She feels that her best is simply not good enough.

Ces told me that the only time her parents praised her was when she graduated *cum laude* in college. But before and after that, not once did they praise her.

Today, shackled by the burden of low self-worth, Ces keeps trying to prove herself to other people. It's creating havoc in her relationships. It's sabotaging her success. Despite her external success, there is so much emptiness in her. Without knowing it, she's desperate for praise, affirmation and love. And when you're emotionally desperate for love, you rarely get love.

The people you love need your praise.

Praise someone today!

CHAPTER 15

Learn to Bless by Speaking It Forth

Every morning, I put my hand on the head of my wife and my two boys. And I say, "God bless you."

Before I leave the house — or before they leave the house — I bless them, too. I place my hand on their forehead and say, "God use you to share His love to others. God protect you." Or sometimes, I just say, "Have a great day today."

Every evening, before they sleep, I give them a blessing, too.

Learn to bless the people in your life.

I lead a large prayer meeting every Sunday. We call it The Feast because thousands come to eat at the rich banquet of God's Word.

But not a few people have told me, "Bo, I go to The Feast because of your preaching, but I also go there because of your blessing. I need it for the week ahead...."

You see, after my talk, I pray for people. I bless the congregation. I extend my hands towards them and say, "God bless you in the next seven days. I pray that God provide for all your needs. I pray that doors of opportunity be opened to you. I pray that you receive a tidal wave of blessings...."

And to people who know the power of a formal blessing, it means the entire world to them.

Now note: There's nothing special about me. I just happen to be the "father" of a spiritual family — that's why my words have power over this group of people.

But you, too, have the exact same power in your tongue.
So make it official.
Speak a formal blessing to *your* family.
Every day.

CHAPTER 16

Prophesy Their Beautiful Future with Your Words

If you've got kids, it's important that you paint a picture of their beautiful future.

Some parents who have temper problems don't get this. They're so flippant with their cruel words, it's maddening. In their rage, they tell their child, "Son, mark my words. You won't amount to anything! You're so irresponsible, you'll end up a bum in the streets."

Of course they don't mean these words. After five minutes, they'll regret what they said. They'll even explain themselves, "Oh, my kids know me. They know my mouth is a loose cannon. Shucks, they don't even listen to me when I'm angry."

But they do! If not consciously, their unconscious mind is drinking it all in and remembering every word, every inflection, forever.

With your words, you're still prophesying their future.

Stop that. Bite your tongue. When you feel your temper rising, step back. Take a few deep breaths. Say a prayer. But never ever speak words that will harm their future.

Instead, start prophesying great things. Fantastic things. Phenomenal things.

Say to them, "You know son, I can see that you will be so successful in life. You will be able to help a lot of people and your life will be so blessed. You're such a wonderful person and I'm so proud of you."

These are the pictures that your children need to see in their future.

By the way, I'm not talking only about children.

With your words, you can prophesy a beautiful future for your spouse, your siblings and your friends.

CHAPTER 17

Use Touch

I've long learned that 87% of communication is non-verbal. Most of it is body language.

So if you want to communicate a blessing to others, learn to touch.

I have a friend who is 37 years old. He told me, "Brother Bo, my father doesn't hug me. But you taught us that if your father doesn't hug you, we should take the initiative and embrace him first."

"That's right," I said.

"Well, I did that. But my dad just brushed me off. So I'm still waiting for him to embrace me after all these years."

I felt so sad for him. My friend carries with him the inner wounds of a father that does not bless him because he does not touch.

I believe that our greatest hunger isn't food. I believe our greatest hunger is for love. And one of the most important ways of receiving that love is through our skin. Our skins hunger for touch.

Make a decision today to touch, to hold hands, to embrace.

When people
around you
curse — turn
a deaf ear.
Transform their
curses to become
your inner fuel
to reach your
goals.

CHAPTER 18

But What If My Family Isn't Blessing Me?

What if your parents haven't blessed you?

What if you're surrounded by people who don't believe in you?

Let me tell you one of my favorite stories.

One day, two frogs fell into a pit.

Frantically, the two frogs cried for help. They kept jumping as high as they could, trying to get out of the hole. But it was just simply beyond their reach.

The other frogs circled at the mouth of the pit. Looking down, they saw the sorry condition of the two frogs, and began to yell, "It's too high. Give up. You're going to die anyway." (They were disciples of Eyeore the Donkey, friend of Winnie the Pooh.) On and on, they chanted their depressing words.

After a few minutes, one frog finally stopped jumping. He sighed a deep sigh, fell on his back and died.

But the other frog kept jumping. And with each leap, he became stronger and stronger. Finally, he flew past the opening of the pit — and escaped!

The other frogs were astonished. They asked him, "Why didn't you give up? It seemed hopeless. We were even discouraging you the entire time!"

The happy frog said, "What did you say? I can't hear you. I was born deaf. By the way, even if I couldn't hear what you were all telling me, I knew you were cheering me on. Thank you!"

Here's the lesson: When people around you curse you — your parents, your siblings, your friends, your teachers, your leaders — turn a deaf ear.

Instead, transform their curses to become your inner fuel to reach your goals.

KEY 4

Proclaim Who You Are

God Never Sees a Failure,
Only a Champion in You

Man is what he believes.
— Anton Chekhov

Problems and promises go together. Your problems are standing in front of the promises of God.

CHAPTER 19

Seeing Only Red in a Sea of Blue

In my talks, I often play this game with the audience.

I ask them to look around the room and count how many red shirts there are.

After half a minute, I tell them to close their eyes. I ask them, "Are you ready with your answer?" They all reply with a resounding yes.

Then I ask them, "OK. How many blue shirts did you see?"

They burst out laughing. And they try to guess. But no one gets the right answer.

Why? Because they weren't focused on the blue shirts but on the red.

The point of this little exercise is to show them that every reality, every situation, every circumstance always has many sides.

But we only see one side! Always.

You're Not a Grasshopper

Let me tell you one of my all-time favorite stories in the Bible.

The Israelites who escaped Egypt (think "Ten Commandments" with Charlton Heston) were now at the edge of the Promised Land. Not knowing what it was like, they sent 12 spies to scout the land if they could conquer it.

When the spies came back, 10 of the 12 gave depressing news. They said, "The land is flowing with milk and honey. But guys, we're no match to the people who live there. They're giants! They're like wrestlers. They'll eat us alive!"

In other words, they only saw red. But the two other spies were named Joshua and Caleb, and they saw blue. They said, "Nonsense! Let's go there now and conquer the land!"

The 10 spies answered back, "Are you crazy? Didn't you see the people there? Compared to them, we're like grasshoppers!"

The Bible says that the rumor spread among the Israelites. And you know how rumors spread. After a while, I bet they were saying, "The people of that land are aliens! They have six legs and two heads! They're 25 feet tall and eat their babies for breakfast."

Soon, all of Israel complained to God for bringing them out of Egypt.

And they stayed in that desert for 40 extra years.

Focus on the Promise, Not on the Problems

Do you feel like your life is on limbo?

That you're in some desert waiting for God's Promise?

Friend, you're at the very edge of God's Promise for your life.

God's miracles are right in front of you.

But you sometimes act like the 10 spies.

You see the Promised Land. You say this is the miracle of God for your life.

But you see the giants and you get scared. You focus on the problems and they become so big, they cover our vision. But understand this: *Problems and promises go together. Your problems are standing in front of the promises of God.* If you have a problem, look behind it and you'll see the promise of God.

Remember that every Promised Land has giants on that land. If there are no giants, then you've got the wrong land.

So you have to learn how to focus on the Promised Land, not the giants in it.

That's why none of the other 10 spies or their descendants entered into the Promised Land. They weren't even able to set foot on it. They circled the wilderness for 40 years until that whole generation died. Only Joshua and Caleb made it in.

God's Promise was delayed for 40 years!

Don't let this happen to your life.

If you want success in life, you have to be vision-oriented, not problem-oriented.

So many leaders are problem-oriented.

Believe me, I've been to leaders' meetings where they meet every week for years and all they talk about are problems in the group, ministry or community.

That group will go nowhere.

Leaders must be men of vision.

They should address the problem as fast as they can so that they can focus on the vision — where God wants them to go and what God wants them to do.

If you want
God's promise
of abundance to
happen in your
life, you have
to dirty your
hands.

CHAPTER 20

Dirty Your Hands

I don't know why the Israelites were shocked when they saw giants in the Promised Land. Maybe they were expecting a welcome committee with a bugle band and huge streamers saying, "Welcome Israelites!" Maybe they expected them to say, "Here, take our homes and our farms. They're all yours!"

Instead, they were greeted by giants. With giant swords and giant shields and giant spears and giant walls surrounding their cities.

To enter God's Promise, they would have to fight.

They'd have to work.

They'd have to hustle.

Friends, if you want God's promise of abundance to happen in your life, you have to dirty your hands.

You want a greater marriage? A more intimate family life? A more successful business? A better job? Stable finances? Better health?

You can't stop at saying that you want it. You have to stand up and work at it!

The Bible says, "All hard work brings a profit, but mere talk leads only to poverty."[1]

Imagine you're thirsty.

And there's a cold glass of water on a table at the other side of the room.

---

[6] Proverbs 14:23

What will you do?

You don't pray and intercede for the glass of water to go near you.

You don't cast it out and say, "I command the spirit of thirst to leave me, in Jesus' name!"

You don't sing, "Come, glass of water, I need you. Come, glass of water, I pray. Come with thy strength and thy power, Come in your own special way…"

No. You actually walk across the room, take the glass in your hand and drink it!

CHAPTER 21

Keep on Doing It, Just Do It a Little Bit Differently

I love the story of Peter's failed fishing expedition.

He told Jesus, "Master, we worked hard all night and caught nothing." In fact, they've been fishing the whole night and couldn't even catch a skinny shrimp.

But Jesus told him, "Lower down your nets one more time. But lower it at the deeper part of the sea."

In my language, Jesus was saying, "Don't give up. Hustle."

And when Peter did as Jesus told him, he received the abundance of the Promised Land. He caught so much fish, the Bible says their nets began to break and their boats almost sank at the weight of the fish.[7]

Friends, if you want a blessing from God, you don't give up. You do whatever it takes to get it. Do what you have to do one more time but do it in a different way. Go deeper. Go higher. Go lower. Just do it.

You know what our problem is?

When we fail, we automatically think we're losers.

No, we're not.

You can never be a loser because you come from God.

Because of that fact, you're a champion.

Always!

---

[7] Luke 5:5-7

When we
mess up, God
still looks for
something good
to look at and
celebrate that
part of us.

CHAPTER 22

The Bias of Fathers

One day, I was at a Christmas party.

Parents were forcing their small kids to sing, bribing them with lollipops to banana splits to doll houses to Boracay vacations.

One father — a friend of mine whose name I won't divulge as it would be hazardous to my health — brought his little five-year-old daughter to the front.

Because he even had a minus one prepared, we thought, "She must really be a good singer." So everyone clapped their hands and cheered as the music started.

That was when the five-year-old began to sing. Or at least made some kind of sharp noise. But she didn't get one key right. The cute little girl was absolutely tone deaf. From beginning to end, she sounded so awful, the experience was similar to having an endoscopy without the anesthesia.

But the father was right beside me, still taking photos, still smiling from ear to ear, his eyes glued to his little daughter. He looked at me and smiled, "She may not sound right but can you see how lovely she sways her hips?"

That's how God sees us: When we mess up, He'll still look for something good to look at and celebrate that part of us.

I've met people who have a terrible image of God. They believe God does nothing else all day but catch them in their sin. Thus, they, too, think of nothing else but their sin.

So I tell them: God sees your goodness before your faults.

Like God, don't focus on your weakness.

Focus on the goodness He created within you.
He doesn't see a failure.
He sees His champion.

Start winning!

KEY 5

Have Trials?
Stand Up and Walk

*Don't Allow Your Problems to Stop You
from Living Life to the Full*

*Man who waits for roast duck to fly into mouth
must wait very, very long time.*
— Chinese Proverb

We have a
human tendency
to blame others
for the trials we
go through.

CHAPTER 23

When You're in a Trial, Stop Blaming Others

A woman wanted to buy a dog.

So she entered a pet store and found a cute puppy for sale.

She told the storeowner, "I'll take him! But I've never had a pet dog before. Can you teach me what to do?"

"It's easy," said the owner. "All you have to do is feed him and bathe him."

"Great!" the woman said as she paid and carried her little puppy home.

The next day, the woman entered the pet store with a dead puppy in her arms.

"You fooled me!" she shouted to the owner. "You never told me that it's bad to soap a puppy when giving him a bath!"

"Huh? What soap did you use?" asked the owner.

"Laundry soap." the woman replied.

"That's a bit strong for the dog but it won't kill him," the owner said. "Please explain to me, step by step, what happened."

The woman said, "First, I held the dog. Second, I put soap on his fur. Third, I put him inside the washing machine and switched it on…"

Poor dog.

Friends, just like that woman, we have a human tendency to blame others for the trials we go through.

When you blame
others, you lose
your power to
determine your
future.

CHAPTER 24

Don't Fix the Blame, Fix the Problem

There was a paralyzed man who lay on his mat for 38 years.[8]

Jesus found him sitting by the Pool of Siloam — a popular healing place.

Their tradition says that the first person to dip into the pool when the water bubbles up will be healed. But since he was paralyzed, someone else would beat him to it.

Instead of taking action, he blamed others.

He said, "I can't get well. No one is helping me." So he just stayed there on his mat year after year after year.

I've met a lot of people like that. They hope for a miracle. But they stay on their mat, blaming others. They stay on their mat, bitter. They stay on their mat, bound to the past.

They blame their parents, their friends, the community, their leaders, their God....

Friend, if you're stuck in your trial, maybe it's because you're stuck in blaming.

Remember this: When you blame others, you lose your power to determine your future. Why? Because you give up the responsibility that God has given you to stand up, pick up your mat and walk.

Don't fix the blame.

Instead, fix the problem.

---

[8] John 5:1-9

I learned that
the problem
child is merely
expressing the
problem of the
marriage.

CHAPTER 25

Learn to Look Within

I was talking to a father who was telling me how terrible his son was. He said, "My son is the most rebellious boy in the world!" On and on, the father ranted, hardly giving me a chance to talk.

So I interrupted him in mid-sentence. "How's your marriage?" I asked.

My question shocked him.

"My marriage?" asked the man, suddenly at a loss for words.

He was quiet for an entire minute. He just stared at me.

Finally, he said, "My marriage is in bad shape. And I'm having an affair."

We had very little time to talk so I unloaded my guns on him. I said, "Your son feels that strain in your marriage. That's why he's rebelling."

Years ago, I took a course in Family Therapy. I learned that the problem child is merely expressing the problem of the marriage. Or the problem of the parents themselves.

So whenever parents bring their problem child to me, I help the parents ask the hard questions, such as, "What am I doing to contribute to the problem? How's my marriage? How's my parenting? How's my personal life?"

Often, that's where the problem lies. Not in the child.

I don't believe
in bad luck. I
believe I create
my luck.

CHAPTER 26

Don't Blame Your Circumstances

Mang Felix is a man who sits on his wooden bench all day.

When I leave the house in the morning, he's already there — sitting outside his home. When I return home in the afternoon, he'd still be on the same spot.

One day, I stopped to chat with him. I found out that he was only 38, younger than I was. I asked him, "*Mang* Felix, if you don't mind me asking, why do you sit here all day? Why don't you work?"

"You know, Brother Bo," he said, "to succeed in life, you need five C's. I only have one."

Hmm. The guy was a philosopher. I asked, "And what are the five C's that you don't have?"

"First, I don't have a *college* degree. I only finished high school. Second, I don't have *capital*. So I can't start a business. The third C is *connections*. I don't have any. The fourth C is *chance*. It's just my destiny to be poor."

I asked, "And what is the one C that you have?"

"I'm cute."

"How about completely catastrophically cataclysmically confused?"

"What?"

"Never mind," I laughed.

"Bo, this is my destiny. But it's OK. I get by. My wife earns a little and we have relatives who help us."

I told Felix, "Do you know Henry Sy, Lucio Tan and John Gokongwei?

He nodded. "Of course, I know them. Who doesn't?"

You're Just Like Henry, John and Lucio

I took a deep breath and began my lecture. "Henry Sy came to the Philippines from China as a young 12-year-old boy with no wealth to speak of except the shirt on his back and the slippers on his feet. At that young age, he worked in a *sari-sari* store 12 hours a day. Today, he owns 27 SM malls all over the country — with 1.6 million people passing through them every single day."

"Wow," Felix muttered.

"John Gokongwei, at the age of 15, was a simple market vendor. He was the youngest market vendor at that time, riding his bicycle, carrying soap, candles and thread. He'd sell them to one customer at a time, face-to-face, belly to belly. He never graduated from college. Today, John Gokongwei is a multi-billionaire and owns Cebu Pacific, Sun Cellular, Robinson's and a host of other businesses."

"Incredible," he shook his head.

"Lucio Tan? Same story. Arrived from China absolutely poor. Never finished college too. But look at him now. He owns Philippine Airlines, Philippine National Bank, Allied Bank, Eton Properties, etcetera. "

"That's great," he said.

"Do you understand?" I asked.

"Understand what?" he asked, his face a total blank.

"They started just like you! Without the C's that you mentioned. *The only difference is that they didn't sit on a wooden bench the whole day.*"

"But I like my wooden bench!" he roared.

"It's never one's destiny to be poor. You may have been born poor but you don't have to *stay* poor."

"But this is my bad luck!" he said, his hand pounding his bench.

"I don't believe in bad luck," I said, as I turned to leave.

"What do you believe in?" he asked.

"I create my luck," I said.

The last time I saw *Mang* Felix, he was still sitting on his wooden bench.

No one is a victim unless you allows yourself to be one.

CHAPTER 27

You're Not a Victim Unless You Allow Yourself to Be One

Every time you're faced with a trial, you have a choice to stay on your mat (or on a wooden bench) and be depressed for the rest of your life.

Felix became comfortable with his poverty to the point that he no longer thought there was anything wrong with it.

Even if your trial is an incurable disease, you still have a choice.

One day, I met a woman who had stage 4 cancer.

When she discovered that she was sick, she stayed in bed all day and cried. But after grieving, she said, "Enough is enough. I need to get up."

Today, this woman lives her life to the hilt. She's a public speaker that travels around the country and gives hope to thousands of people. She's just amazing.

I met her again recently — and she's still at it. If you look at her, you wouldn't suspect she had cancer at all.

Because in her mind, she isn't a cancer victim.

No one is a victim unless you allow yourself to be one.

Nothing can stop you from living life with joy.

Play Ball!

Another friend of mine learned that his kidneys were failing.

"My creatinine level is so high, the doctor says there's no hope of bringing it down," he said with a sad voice. "Unless I go through dialysis or have a kidney transplant, my doctor says I only have six months to live."

That day, we prayed together for his healing.

A year later, I saw him again. He was alive and I was amazed at how he changed. His body was so lean and firm, he looked like an athlete!

"What happened to you?" I asked.

"Bo," he replied, "remember my doctor said that my creatinine level won't go down anymore? We'll, it went down. In fact, it's normal now."

"What did you do?" I asked.

"Aside from all the prayers, I began playing badminton every day."

I blinked, wondering if I heard him right. "Badminton?"

"Yes! Every day, I play with my wife and kids. For four hours, I sweat like crazy."

My friend didn't sit on a mat the whole day.

If You Don't Like the Show, Change the Channel

Imagine a guy complaining about what's on TV. He says, "Oh, this is a terrible show. I hate it. I just don't like the characters. The acting is bad. It's so boring. Ugh... I hate this show!"

So you tell the guy, "Hey, change the channel."

"I can't," he says, "the remote is busted."

"Well, how about walking to the TV and changing the channel?" you suggest.

"Oh, that's just too much work," he replies.

Friends, if you don't like what you're seeing in your life, don't suffer through it. Pick yourself up from the couch, walk to the TV set of life and change the channel.

Here's what I realized about life: We don't have a remote control in our hand.

There's none.

We've got to stand up, walk and get healed.

If you tell yourself, "My trial is just too much. It'll kill me." Guess what? You really will die because that's your faith.

CHAPTER 28

The Power of Your Mind

You know how powerful your mind is?

I'll show you with a true story.

Nick worked in a railroad company.

One summer, he accidentally locked himself in a refrigerated car.

He screamed and banged on the door but his coworkers had already gone home.

No one could hear Nick's desperate cry for help.

Because he knew it was a refrigerated boxcar, he guessed that the temperature was well below freezing. He tried to find an opening to get out but the car was sealed shut.

So he lay down on the floor, shivering.

Slowly, he felt he was dying.

He was able to peel off part of the flooring. With a sharp instrument, he began writing on the wood underneath. "Getting so cold, body numb. If I don't get out soon, these may be my last words," he wrote.

The next morning, they opened the boxcar and found Nick's dead body crumpled over in the corner. When the autopsy was completed, it revealed that Nick had indeed frozen to death.

Here's the mystery: The freezer in the boxcar wasn't even on!

It had been busted for some time. The temperature in the car that night was 16 degrees Celsius. That's just like Baguio[9] temperature!

---

[9] Baguio is a mountain city—the summer capital of the Philip-

But because he *believed* he was freezing, his body obeyed. His internal organs obeyed. And they froze to death. He expected to die and he did.

Nick lost the battle in his own mind.

If you're lying down on your mat and you tell yourself, "My trial is just too much. It'll kill me." Guess what? You really will die because that's your faith.

So I want you to have a new kind of faith. Tell yourself, "Through this trial, God is telling me, 'Stand up, pick up your mat, and walk!'"

KEY 6

Take Out the Trash

Remove the Clogs from Your Heart That Prevent the Easy Flow of Blessings

Watch out that no poisonous root of bitterness grows up to trouble you, corrupting many.
— Hebrews 12:15

If you want
to live a life
of miracles,
unforgiveness is
one thing that
must be thrown
away.

Chapter 29

Get Rid of the Dirt of Unforgiveness

A mother and his four-year-old boy were brushing their teeth together.

Suddenly, the little boy's toothbrush slipped from his hand and it fell right into the toilet bowl. Instinctively, the boy reached in the toilet, fished out his toothbrush and was about to put it into his mouth again when the mother shrieked to the highest heavens.

"STOP!" Immediately, she grabbed the toothbrush from her son and threw it into the trash bin.

After washing her son's hand and giving him a new toothbrush, they continued brushing their teeth. The little boy asked, "Mom, why did you throw away my old toothbrush?"

"Because it's dirty! It fell into the toilet," explained the mother.

"Oh," the boy said. "Mom, I think you also have to throw away your toothbrush."

"Why?" the mother asked as she continued to brush her teeth.

"'Because three days ago, I dropped your toothbrush in the toilet bowl. But I got it back and returned it!"

If it's dirty, it has to be thrown away.

But I know many people who still keep spiritual trash in their lives.

One of them is unforgiveness.

If you want to live a life of miracles, this is one thing that must be thrown away.

CHAPTER 30

Allow Yourself to Be Angry

I'm not saying you can't be angry.

I've learned that forgiveness is a journey of three specific parts. The first part is to face the anger. To acknowledge the anger. To validate it. To admit that you've been wronged. The second is to pray for the power to forgive. And the third is to release that anger and forgive.

When someone hurts you very deeply, you can't just say, "That's OK. Forget about it. It's all water under the bridge." No. You need to tell yourself, "It's OK to be angry." Let me tell you why.

In my books *Your Past Does Not Define Your Future* and *7 Secrets to Real Freedom,* I wrote about my childhood experience of being sexually molested by two men. And how it caused me to have a porn addiction that almost destroyed my life.

For the longest time, as a teenager, I thought I had already forgiven these men. "It's easy for me to forgive," I'd tell people when they ask me about it. What I didn't realize was that I wasn't facing the anger in my soul.

Years later, I realized that because I didn't allow myself to get angry, I wasn't giving value to myself. In other words, I wasn't loving myself. Which was important for my inner healing and the healing of my addictions.

No wonder I couldn't control the addictions that were raging within me. It was my soul crying out for love, but because it wasn't getting any, it escaped to substitutes for love. For me, it was porn and sexual fantasies.

But the day I finally acknowledged that what these men did to me was wrong — a horrible crime — and that I was angry at what they did — I felt valued! And it was the start of my healing.

CHAPTER 31

But Don't Let Anger Last Too Long

There's a story of two monks, Big Monk and Small Monk. They were walking in the woods when they saw a pretty woman at the edge of a river. She asked, "Can you help me cross the bridge?"

Big Monk immediately said yes. He carried her in his arms, crossed the bridge and put her down on the other side.

Small Monk was furious! He told himself, "How could this monk do this? We're not allowed to even touch a woman, much less a pretty woman at that, and he even carried her in his arms!"

He didn't say anything, but after eight long hours of walking, he finally burst out in anger, "I thought you were a holy monk? How could you have done that? You carried that woman in your arms!"

The big monk said, "I carried that woman for one minute. When I put her down by the river, I left her there. You, however, have been carrying her in your mind for the past eight hours."

Sometimes we can be like Small Monk.

When we have anger in our hearts, we make it last.

You can
deal with
unforgiveness
in the heart if
you have a good
relationship
and you're able
to lovingly and
gently share
those moments
when you were
hurt.

CHAPTER 32

A Marriage Tip That Can Save You Years of Heartache

My wife and I have a great marriage. But people get shocked when I tell them that we fight about maybe five, six times a day.

But our fights last only for a minute.

We've vowed to each other that we won't hide our little irritations. It's better to be honest and upfront — rather than let this anger build up for weeks or months — and explode like Mt. Pinatubo whose last eruption was 600 years before its most recent one. That's why it was so deadly.

If I get irritated by something she does, I just tell her, "Sweetheart, I was hurt with what you did." And she'd say, "Oh, I'm sorry." And that's it.

Some keep it inside and carry it for hours, days or months until they become historical and hysterical. They scream at each other, "Do you remember, in 1967, when you did this…?" And the history lessons go on.

You can deal with unforgiveness in the heart if you have a good relationship and you're able to lovingly and gently share those moments when you were hurt.

That's why it's important to work through the feelings right away, face your anger, acknowledge it and let it pass.

Forgiveness is, first of all, a gift I give myself.

CHAPTER 33

Get the Grace to Be Gracious

The second part of the journey of unforgiveness is to pray to God for the power to forgive.

When I made the decision to forgive my abusers, I realized a powerful thing: Forgiveness is, first of all, a gift I give myself.

Because when I forgave, I was released from my abuser's power. As long as I didn't forgive, I remained in the clutches of my abuser.

Do you want to know when you have really forgiven?

When you hear bad news about that person's life and you do not gloat over his misfortune. You do not say, "Oh, good for him! After all he's done to me, he deserves it." No, that just means you still haven't forgiven.

When you wish that your enemy be cursed, I warn you, the curse comes back to you. Because what you sow, you reap.

But when you've reached the third part of the journey of forgiveness — actually pardoning the person — and you've made that decision in your mind, even if your emotions lag behind your decisions, you can sincerely say, "I pray that this person will be blessed by God."

You may ask, "Bo, is that humanly possible?"

My answer is no. But that's what part two of the journey is for. We ask the Lord for the power to forgive.

In this journey of forgiveness, you cannot skip parts, especially if the hurt is very deep.

Wish blessing
upon those who
hurt you — and
that blessing will
come back to
you!

CHAPTER 34

An Amazing Story of Forgiveness

Let me tell you the story of my friend Charlie.

Charlie is a businessman who put up a successful restaurant in Hong Kong.

Because he found it difficult to hire locals, he employed Filipino domestic helpers instead. Later on, he learned that this was illegal. According to Hong Kong law, domestic helpers were supposed to work in homes, not in restaurants.

Charlie wanted to fix the problem. But since he paid them well, his employees didn't want to leave the company. So Charlie made a deal with five of them. He said, "Why don't you go back to the Philippines, apply for the proper working visa, and I'll sponsor you?"

But the Hong Kong Embassy rejected all their applications.

With a heavy heart, Charlie had to let them go — but not without giving them a generous separation pay. He wanted them to have some seed money to start a business in the Philippines.

But during this same time, Charlie had a conflict with one of his managers.

Out of spite, this manager instigated the dismissed employees to turn against Charlie. So they all filed a case against him: That he hired them against Hong Kong law for years. After a yearlong trial, Charlie was sentenced to 22 months in jail.

Charlie was crushed. He felt like a wrecker ball fell on his life.

On his first night in jail, he curled up in his bunk, covered himself with a blanket, and cried. He couldn't even pray. He shed tears of grief for being separated from his family and tears of fury for those who betrayed him.

But as the days went by, he heard God's gentle invitation in the depths of his heart — "Forgive."

Charlie struggled with this word. How could he forgive those who betrayed him after all the years of helping them? How could he forgive that one person — the manager — who convinced his employees to sue him?

But Charlie realized that he couldn't remain angry forever. He knew it was going to poison him. He trusted in the justice of the Lord. He let go and let God.

After a few months, Charlie was released.

Today, he continues to serve the Lord as a successful businessman — free from the bitterness that would have prevented the blessings of God to flow into his life.

Don't Let Anyone Steal Your Blessings

Do you nurture anger towards anyone who has hurt you?

Then you're letting them steal your blessings.

Why are you doing that?

If they hurt you, then why allow them to hurt you more with your own resentments? When you seek to punish those who harmed you, you're really punishing yourself.

Friend, let go. In fact, wish blessing upon those who hurt you — and that blessing will come back to you!

KEY 7

Sow in Times of Famine

Learn One of the Most Powerful Laws of Abundance

God loves a cheerful giver.
— 2 Corinthians 9:7

God has given every blessing you need in your life already. That tank has your name on it. It's yours! All you have to do is open the faucet.

Chapter 35

Laws of the Universe

Throw a basketball up in the air.

What happens? It falls down.

Because of the Law of Gravity.

That's what my Science Teacher told me in grade school. She said, "You can't see it. You can't touch it. But the Law of Gravity is there."

Now try this out at home.

Pick up any ball and say over and over again, "I don't believe in gravity, I don't believe in gravity, I don't believe in gravity!" Say it with feeling. Say it with deep conviction. Shout it out while jumping up and down.

Then throw the ball up in the air.

What happens? It *still* falls!

The Law of Gravity works every time, no exceptions.

It doesn't matter if you believe in this law or not.

It doesn't matter if you're a good person or not.

It doesn't matter if you're close to God or not.

I repeat: The Law of Gravity works every time.

You Harvest What You Plant

Friends, there's another law as universal as the Law of Gravity. It's called the Law of Giving. The Bible says, *"You will always harvest what you plant."*[10]

---

[10] Galatians 6:7

If I plant one mango seed and it becomes a tree, that tree will give me 6,000 mango fruits in its lifetime. So if I plant two mango seeds, I'll harvest 12,000 mangoes. The more I plant, the more I harvest. It's that simple.

If I smile rarely, I'll receive smiles rarely, too. If I smile a lot, I'll receive a lot of smiles, too.

That's why the Bible says, "Give, and you will receive. The amount you give will determine the amount you get back."[11]

Again, it doesn't matter if I believe in this law or not.

What you give, you receive more.

That's just how the universe works.

Now why am I explaining this to you?

God's Blessings Are Waiting for You

Let's correct a silly idea. Some people think that God is in heaven, sitting on His throne, watching and waiting for someone to give money in the love offering basket. And when He sees someone giving, he tosses him a blessing. "Here's your candy, boy! Good work!" He says.

Believe me, that's *not* how it works.

Instead, I believe God has already rigged the universe with the Law of Giving, in the same way that He has rigged the universe with the Law of Gravity. (When you toss a ball up in the air, God doesn't have to push the ball down with His finger every time, right?)

Instead, the Law of Giving is written in every atom of God's creation.

So imagine a gigantic tank of blessings that's filled to the brim. God has given every blessing you need in your life already. That tank has your name on it. It's yours!

All you have to do is open the faucet.

And one of the ways of opening the faucet is giving.

---

[11] Luke 6:38

CHAPTER 36

The "Problem" with Tithing
as It Is Taught Today

But I have a little problem with how tithing is being preached today.

I simply don't believe that you should give to God because of fear of being cursed. Instead, you should tithe because you love.

Some preachers *scare* people to tithe by quoting Malachi 3. They read, "Dare a man rob God? Yet you are robbing me! And you say, 'How do we rob you?' In tithes and in offerings! You are indeed accursed, for you, the whole nation, rob me. Bring the whole tithe into the storehouse..." But this is tithing seen as an Old Testament law. There's a tithing that's of the New Testament, and there's a nuance I want you to see.

God Isn't a Tyrant

What if my mother, Pilar, told me, "Bo, give me money. Or I won't talk to you again. In fact, I will put you under a curse." What kind of parent is that? She won't be nominated for the Mother of the Year Award, that's for sure. But that's exactly how we imagine God to be!

Instead, I believe that Malachi is speaking about the natural consequences of violating a specific law of the universe.

Let me give you an analogy.

Do this experiment in your spare time. Try jumping off the 30th floor of your office building but be sure your insurance is up-to-date.

105

Will it hurt a bit? Unless you're Spiderman, absolutely. Simply because you're not "following" the Law of Gravity.

Now God doesn't have to enter the picture, does He? He doesn't have to say, "Aha! You're not following the Law of Gravity! You're cursed!" and with His finger poking from the sky, He flicks your body down to your death on the pavement below.

Gravity takes care of that.

Same thing with giving. When you give or don't give, there are natural consequences that *just* happen. No "supernatural" intervention necessary.

Why Do You Give?

Here's my point: I'm not saying you shouldn't tithe. You should! There is such a thing as New Testament tithing. But you should throw away the idea that God will curse you if you don't tithe. Don't tithe because you fear. Tithe because you love.

Going back to my example above, yes, I give to my Mom. She doesn't have to force me to give by threatening with a curse. Why? Because I love her. It's my great joy to give her money.

Sacrificial Giving

If you're going to ask me, "Bo, what kind of giving is taught by the New Testament?" I'll answer, "Tithing is great. But more than tithing, it calls us to sacrificial giving."

Here's the passage from the New Testament: "And don't give reluctantly or in response to pressure. For God loves a person who gives cheerfully."[12]

Do you see the difference from the Old Testament's threat of a curse?

---

[12] 2 Corinthians 9:6-8

If you ask me, "Bo, what percentage am I going to give?" I'll still say, "Start with 10%. It's a wonderful guideline." But from its very definition, sacrificial giving is something that you must decide from your heart — not because you're pressured, not because of fear, not because you're forced to give.

Give sacrificially.

Not to earn brownie points with God.

Not to avoid curses.

But because you love.

It isn't the percentage that matters but how much is left after you give.

CHAPTER 37

It's Not How Much You Give But How Much Is Left Behind

Sacrificial giving is not so much about the percentage you're giving but the amount left after you give.

Let me illustrate this point for you.

Jose earns P5,000 a month and gives P500 to God.

Carlos earns P50,000 and gives P5,000 to God.

Now tell me, who has given the most to God?

It's easy to say Carlos, because he gave P5,000, right?

But from a spiritual vantage point, Jose gave the most — even if he only gave P500.

Why? Both Jose and Carlos gave 10% of their earnings. But when Carlos gave P5,000, he still had P45,000 left. When Jose gave his P500, he only had P4,500 left. In his poverty, he still gave to God. Jose was *sowing in time of famine.*

Carlos *tithed,* but Jose gave *sacrificially.*

His was the biggest gift of all.

Friends, it isn't the percentage that matters but how much is left after you give.

Tithing is the training wheels of giving.

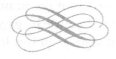

CHAPTER 38

Three Practical Steps to Take

Step #1: Make a decision on how much you're going to give to God.
Yes, 10% is still a great model to follow. Tithing is the training wheels of giving. Start there. But remember not to do it because of fear or external pressure but because you love.

Step #2: Make your giving your first expense.
Don't pay your bills and give what's leftover. Believe me, nothing will be leftover! God has to be first, so your monthly offering must be your first expense.

Step #3: Pray for abundance and desire to give more.
Ask God to bless you more. Increase your financial literacy. Your savings must be your second expense. Learn how to invest. Learn how to increase your income and have many income streams. And as your blessings increase, give more to God. Increase your giving to 11%, and then 12%, and then 13%... and so on!

Do you want to know one of my dreams? When I get older, I want to do a "reverse tithe." I want to give 90% of my income and keep the 10% for my needs.

Do you want to join me?

The happiest people in the world are givers.

Chapter 39

Four Reasons for Giving

Let me end this chapter with why sowing in time of famine (sacrificial giving) is the only way to live a life of miracles. Here are four reasons for giving:

1. When you give, you're happy.
   Show me a giving person and I'll show you a happy person. The happiest people in the world are givers.

2. When you give, you gain an abundance mentality.
   Giving takes you out of your scarcity mentality — and makes you realize that we live in a generous universe. Giving breaks your poverty thinking — that you are not poor after all.

3. When you give, you grow in love.
   If you give, you don't have to love. But if you love, you have to give.

4. When you give, you get blessed.
   Because it's a law built into this universe.

If you want to live a life of miracles, learn to sow in time of famine.

Happy giving, my friends!

Epilogue

My Mom Lives a Life of Miracles

I began this book with the love story of Mom and Dad.

I'll end this book with a continuation of that love story.

In 1996, my father had a major accident.

When he was 76 years old, he changed a light bulb in our garage. To reach it, he stepped on a little bench. But he lost his balance and crashed his head on the hard concrete floor. Instantly, blood flowed like an open faucet.

We rushed him to the hospital. Through a CT scan, they found three blood clots in his brain. After two brain surgeries, he lost his clear eyesight and damaged his emotional center. He spent five months in the ICU. We thought he was dying. But God extended his life for another 12 years.

But those 12 years were difficult. He was no longer the Dad we knew. He used to be a tower of strength and stability. Now, he was moody, erratic and even childish. And through all those 12 years, it was my mom who was there for him. He may have changed but she didn't. Her love for him was as strong as ever.

She served him with special devotion.

She cared for him 24 hours a day, seven days a week.

Because he walked unsteadily, she held his arm wherever they went.

Because he could no longer read, she read aloud to him every day.

Because he grumbled most of the time, she listened to him with patience.

When Dad reached 88, he went home to the Lord.

Mom was devastated. The love of her life, her companion of 63 years, was gone. To this day, at different times, I still find her crying.

In the meantime, she faced her own trials.

Recently, Mom suffered a mild stroke that affected her memory. Initially, she couldn't remember proper names.

One time, she went to church. After Mass, she rode a tricycle to go home. But when the tricycle driver asked where she lived, she couldn't remember her street.

Lapses like that make life difficult for her.

Here's my point.

With all her trials, Mom could have chosen to live miserably.

She could just think of herself, be selfish and sink into depression.

She didn't do any of these.

Instead, she decided to be happy.

Yes, she decided to live a life of miracles.

Let me tell you how.

An 80-Plus-Year-Old Woman Lives Like She's 40

Once, my wife and I were in the car with her.

During the drive, she started reading the newspaper.

My wife asked, "Mom, why are you reading in the car? You'll get dizzy!"

Mom's reply struck me. She said, "You know, I have no time to read the newspaper at home. I'm so busy!"

Friends, that line came from an 83-year-old woman!

Let me describe the exciting miracles she does.

She serves Anawim, our home for the abandoned elderly, helping out donors who want to visit our Center in Montalban. With love and her knack for meticulous detail, she'll talk about Anawim, its history, its various needs and how they can help.

For years now, she transformed her home to become a tiny bookstore to sell my books — so that every day, she can entertain a steady stream of book lovers. She doesn't just sell books. If you give her a chance, she'll even narrate the entire book to you, you won't even have to buy it.

Mom also has a beautiful telephone ministry that spans the entire world. And at 83, she has an active text ministry. (Yes, she uses SMS like she was a high school girl.) She reaches out, builds relationships and touches lives.

She also loves going with me to my seminars and foreign trips. Just to talk to people. To be there. To smile.

Last year, she went to the US with me. Two months ago, we went to Indonesia and Singapore. Next year, we'll be traveling together to another part of the world.

I repeat: She has trials.

But each day, she lives an exciting life of miracles.

A life a 40-year-old will envy.

There Are Miracles Everywhere!

I hope you learned these three powerful truths in this book:

1. You are a miracle.
2. You live in a world of miracles.
3. And every day, you can create miracles.

Thank you for reading my book.

As usual, I didn't share just my thoughts.

It was a great pleasure sharing my life with you.

I hope to see you soon.

Bo Sanchez

PS. Get more inspiration through my FREE *Soulfood* Letter. Sign up at **www.BoSanchez.ph** now!

PS2. To get a complete spiritual support system for your life, log on to **www.KerygmaFamily.com.** You'll get FREE daily Bible reflections and digital copies of our inspiring magazines!

PS3. To receive practical wisdom on growing your financial life and spiritual life at the same time, log on to **www.IAmTrulyRich. com** and sign up for my FREE *TrulyRich* Letter.

Grow in Your Financial Life and Spiritual Life at the Same Time

Learn up-to-date, cutting-edge information on how you can make your money work for you and create passive income. Receive Bo Sanchez's Truly Rich Letter. In it, you will find...

- Advice on where to put your money for long-term growth
- How to know if an investment is good or not good
- Marketing strategies that will consistently grow your small business
- What are the wrong financial habits that rob you of your wealth
- How to remain spiritually strong as your money increases
- So much more!

Log on to www.IAmTrulyRich.com and receive Bo Sanchez's TrulyRich Letter. Don't miss this great storehouse of financial wisdom that can save you from financial ruin and misery.

About the Author

Bo Sanchez is the author of 13 bestselling books and publisher of seven magazines. Bo also has a weekly TV show, a daily radio program, and a daily Internet show. He travels extensively around the world as a powerful speaker. So far, he has addressed audiences in 14 countries, including 37 cities in North America. His Soulfood blog is read each week by more than a hundred thousand people. You can read his blog at **www.BoSanchez.ph** and his video blog at **www. PreacherInBlueJeans.com**

He founded many organizations, such as Anawim, a special home for the abandoned elderly, and Shepherd's Voice, a media group that publishes the widest read inspirational literature in the country. He also founded an international, borderless, virtual, on-line community called **www.KerygmaFamily.com** that helps people grow in their spiritual life.

Bo received The Outstanding Young Men (TOYM) Award for 2006 and the Serviam Award, the highest recognition given by CMMA or Catholic Mass Media Awards.

Privately, Bo is also a micro-entrepreneur. He engages in small business and real estate not only for his family's needs and for his various projects, but also from his firm belief that one of the most important solutions to his country's economic problems is to raise up more micro-entrepreneurs among his countrymen. He frequently teaches and writes about financial literacy, believing that our poverty is hugely a product of people's low financial I.Q. on subjects such as debt-management, saving, investing and

Bo with son Bene

business. He writes the TrulyRich Letter at **www.IAmTrulyRich. com** to help people grow in their financial life and spiritual life at the same time.

In another endeavor he's passionate about, Bo started the Catholic Filipino Academy to help parents who want to teach their children at home. For more information, log on to **www. CatholicFilipinoAcademy.com**

But above all these, Bo believes that his first call is to be a loving husband to his wife, Marowe, and a devoted father to his sons, Benedict and Francis. They live in Manila, Philippines.

Start your day right. Every day.

Subscribe now!

- ☐ Didache P120 ☐ Gabay P120
- ☐ Companion P480 *Freight cost P100 (provincial)*
- ☐ Sabbath (1 year) P250 *Freight cost P75 (provincial)*

ORDER FORM

Name: _____ B-day: _____

Address: _____

Telephone number(s): _____ Date sent: _____

E-mail address: _____

☐ Cash ☐ Check ☐ Money Order

☐ Bank deposit thru BDO S/A No. 397-000070-4

or BPI S/A No. 0123-4832-94, Allied Bank S/A No. 3160-00255-7,

Metrobank S/A No. 3-2655-0807-4 (validated deposit slip enclosed)

☐ I am authorizing Equitable Card Network to charge my Visa/Mastercard

in the amount of P _____

Card number: ☐☐☐☐ ☐☐☐☐ ☐☐☐☐ ☐☐☐☐

Expiry date: _____

Signature: _____

Last 3 digits at back of the card ☐☐☐

Please allow 4-5 weeks for delivery of your first copy. If you don't receive your purchase after 5 weeks, please call Customer Service at (02)726-9918/411-7874 to 77.

• *Prices are subject to change without prior notice.*

SUBSCRIBE TO KERYGMA!

Inspiring You to Live a Fantastic Life!

Bo Sanchez is the main writer of KERYGMA, the #1 Inspirational Magazine in the country. Get a whole year subscription of 12 exciting issues for only P640 . Feed your soul with God's Word at this affordable price!

Call us at (632) 411-78-74 to 77 or email us at sale@shepherds-voice.com.ph, or write to Shepherd's Voice, #60 Chicago St., Cubao, Quezon City 1109. Check out our website at www.shepherdsvoice.com.ph or fill up the order form below.

Subscribe now! You'll be blessed 12 times a year!

ORDER FORM

Name: _____ B-day: _____

Address: _____

Telephone number(s): _____ Date sent: _____

E-mail address: _____

❑ Cash   ❑ Check   ❑ Money Order

❑ Bank deposit thru BDO S/A No. 397-000070-4

or BPI S/A No. 0123-4832-94, Allied Bank S/A No. 3160-00255-7,

Metrobank S/A No. 3-2655-0807-4 (validated deposit slip enclosed)

❑ I am authorizing Equitable Card Network to charge my Visa/Mastercard

in the amount of P _____

Card number: ☐☐☐☐ ☐☐☐☐ ☐☐☐☐ ☐☐☐☐

MasterCard

VISA

Expiry date: _____

Signature: _____

Last 3 digits at back of the card ☐☐☐

ORDERING IS EASY!

• By Fax : fax this form to 7275615 or 7269918

• By Mail: return this form with your payment (PMO or check payable to Shepherd's Voice) 60 Chicago St., Cubao, Quezon City

Prices are subject to change without prior notice.

OTHER BOOKS BY BO SANCHEZ

THE BOSS Series
How to Be Really, Really, Really Happy (First Collection)
You Can Make Your Life Beautiful (Second Collection)
You Have the Power to Create Love (Third Collection)
Fill Your Life with Miracles (Fourth Collection)

SIMPLIFY Series
Simplify and Live the Good Life
Simplify and Create Abundance

PRAYERBOOKS
Embraced
The Way of the Cross
Special Prayers for the Holy Rosary

Your Past Does Not Define Your Future
How to Find Your One True Love
How to Find Your One True Love Book 2
8 Secrets of the Truly Rich
7 Secrets to Real Freedom
40 Stories of Passion
Eagles Don't Fly... They Soar!

SHEPHERD'S
V O I C E

Learn to live a fantastic life. Log on to www.bosanchez.ph